SEVEN and a half TONS of Steel

A POST-9/11 STORY OF HOPE AND TRANSFORMATION

Janet Nolan

Illustrated by
Thomas Gonzalez

PEACHTREE
ATLANTA

THERE IS A SHIP, a navy ship. It is called the USS *New York*. It is big like other navy ships, and it sails like other navy ships, but there is something different, something special about the USS *New York*.

On September 11, 2001, clouds of smoke billowed into the clear blue sky. The World Trade Center towers came down. Almost three thousand people lost their lives.

In the days after the towers collapsed,
people brought flowers and photographs,
stuffed animals and pictures drawn
with crayon. They lit candles and left
handwritten notes to decorate a place
now called Ground Zero.

For weeks and months afterward,
people cleared away metal and stone
from Ground Zero. One truck carried
a beam, made of steel, from
New York to a foundry
in Louisiana.

Workers heated the beam to a high, high temperature. Steel melted into liquid. Molten metal, bright orange and fiery red, was poured into a mold. It took four days to cool.

Seven and a half tons of steel,
which had once been a beam
in the World Trade Center,
was now the bow of a navy
ship. Chippers and grinders,
painters and polishers
worked on it for months.

Once a beam, but now a bow,
it was taken to a shipyard in the
city of New Orleans. Shipbuilders,
engineers, electricians, mechanics,
welders, carpenters, painters,
and plumbers worked together
to build the USS *New York*.

And then it was time
to install the bow.

Shipbuilders stopped their work and
came to watch. Draped in an American flag,
seven and a half tons of steel were lifted
by a crane and welded into place
on the USS *New York*.

Out in the ocean, a storm started to swirl.
Wind twisted. Water churned.

Hurricane Katrina slammed into New Orleans.
Levees broke, homes flooded, and
businesses were swept away.

Many shipbuilders lost their homes.
They could not work on the
USS *New York* until…

Kamp Katrina was built.

Now the workers had a place to live. They could continue building the ship.

Finally, the USS *New York* was finished.
But the mighty ship still sat on dry land.

Inch by inch, using skids, grease, and
hydraulic lifts, the ship was put into
the water. It was the biggest moving
object on the earth that day.

The ship sailed down the Mississippi,
into the Gulf of Mexico, and out into
the open waters of the Atlantic Ocean.

The USS *New York* was going home.

The USS *New York* sailed past the Statue of Liberty and came to a stop across from Ground Zero, the site where the World Trade Center towers once stood. There was silence on the water. There was silence on the land.

The silence was broken by a twenty-one-gun salute.

When the ceremony ended,
the warship set out to do
its job at sea.

On September 11, 2011, the tenth anniversary of the collapse of the World Trade Center towers, the USS *New York* returned home. The men and women of the United States military services lined the rails of the ship. People came from all over the country and around the world to see the ship that bore the crest "Never Forget."

The USS *New York* is part of our American history. Wherever it sails the high seas, its bow cuts the water.

Seven and a half tons of steel lead the way.

More about the USS *New York*

LENGTH: 684 feet

WEIGHT: 25,000 tons

CONTAINS: 500 miles of electrical cable, 315 tons of paint, 60 miles of piping

SPEED: up to 22 knots (about 25 miles per hour)

MOTTO: "Strength forged through sacrifice. Never forget." On the crest it is shortened to "Never Forget."

The USS *New York* was built to carry up to 360 U.S. Navy sailors and 700 to 800 combat-ready Marine Corps troops, their equipment, and supplies.

The USS *New York* is also known as LPD 21. LPD stands for "landing platform/dock." The USS *New York* is the 21st LPD in the navy's fleet.

On the ship, there is a diner called the Skyline Café, which was the name of a restaurant in the World Trade Center.

The crest of the USS *New York*

The crest features three colors

★ Dark blue and gold: the sea and excellence (Navy colors)

★ Red: sacrifice and valor

★ White: purity of purpose

On the crest, you'll find the following elements, which represent

★ Blue border: the New York State Seal

★ Sunburst: the Statue of Liberty

★ Mountain and lake, surrounded by maple leaves: the state of New York

★ Crossed swords: the Navy and Marine Corps

★ Gray bars: Twin Towers

★ Gray chevron: the bow of the ship. This intersects with the gray bars to indicate that the bow of the ship incorporates steel from the World Trade Center.

★ Three stars: battle stars earned by a previous USS *New York* during World War II

★ Phoenix: the country's hope and determination. On the shield on the phoenix's breast

- Red stripe: the New York City Fire Department
- Dark blue stripe: the New York City Police Department
- Light blue stripe: the Port Authority of New York and New Jersey
- Red drops: blood and sacrifice

Ω

PEACHTREE PUBLISHING COMPANY INC.

1700 Chattahoochee Avenue
Atlanta, Georgia 30318-2112
www.peachtree-online.com

Illustrations created in pastel, colored pencil,
and watercolor on archival 100% rag watercolor paper.
Title created with Pilsen Plaket by Dieter Steffmann for
Typographer Mediengestaltung, 2000; text typeset in
ITC Bookman by Ed Benguiat for International Typeface
Corporation.

Edited by Kathy Landwehr
Title, book, and jacket designed by Thomas E. Gonzalez;
composition by Loraine M. Joyner

Printed in May 2021 by Toppan Leefung Printing Limited
in China
10 9 8 7 6 5 (hardcover)
10 9 8 7 6 5 4 3 2 1 (paperback)

HC ISBN: 978-1-56145-912-4
PB ISBN: 978-1-68263-328-1

Library of Congress Cataloging-in-Publication Data

Title: Seven and a half tons of steel / written by Janet
Nolan ; illustrated by Thomas Gonzalez.
Description: Atlanta, GA : Peachtree Publishers, [2016]
Identifiers: LCCN 2015046214
Subjects: LCSH: New York (Amphibious transport dock:
LPD-21)—Juvenile literature. | September 11 Terrorist
Attacks, 2001—Influence—Juvenile literature.
Classification: LCC VA65.N616 N65 2016 | DDC
623.825/6—dc23 LC record available at
http://lccn.loc.gov/2015046214

To the men and women who
built and who serve on the
USS *New York*

—J. N.

I would like to dedicate my
work to my family, to our
founding fathers, and to all
who perished on 9/11.

—T. G.